my first CAMERA BOOK

By Anne Kostick • Illustrated by Tedd Arnold

100% LOYAL BIALOSKY & FRIENDS AND TRUE

WORKMAN PUBLISHING, NEW YORK

Library of Congress
Cataloging-in-Publication Data

Kostick, Anne.
    My first camera book.

    "100% loyal and true Bialosky &
    friends."
    Includes index.
    Summary: Teddy bear Bialosky
shares his secrets for taking good pictures
and suggests projects such as making
postcards, puzzles, and decorated photo
albums.
    1. Photography—Juvenile literature.
[1. Photography] I. Arnold, Tedd, ill.
II Title.
TR149.K67   1989   771   88-40560
ISBN 0-89480-381-6

Cover and book design by Tedd Arnold

Workman Publishing Company, Inc.
708 Broadway
New York, NY 10003

Printed in the United States of America
First printing June 1989
10   9   8   7   6

Contents

A Note From Bialosky Bear

Hi! My name is Bialosky Bear, and I love to take pictures. Shooting pictures with your own camera is lots of fun when you know how. You can use snapshots to remember great events, tell stories, and share your life with friends who live far away. This book will show you how to shoot a good photograph with the simple camera included in the package. As you grow older, you'll probably take pictures with bigger, fancier cameras, but the rules of good picture taking will stay the same. Only the buttons and dials on the camera will change. You may need an adult's help at first to load the camera or advance the film, but soon you'll be doing everything yourself, and their only job will be to pose for pictures. Then you'll be a real "shutterbug," like me!

Happy snapping, *Bialosky*

Photography

Photography is a way of making pictures out of what you see in the world around you. Instead of

painting with brushes and paint, photographers use a camera, film, and light to make a picture. First the camera captures the picture, and the film stores it. Then a photo lab prints the picture on special paper, which is all white at first but changes into a colorful photograph when light hits it.

Machines may do much of the work, but a lot of it depends on the photographer—you! What you choose to put in your picture, how you use light and shadow, or how you arrange close-up and faraway things can make the difference between a good photograph and a very good photograph.

ABOUT YOUR CAMERA

Some cameras, like yours, are simple to work, and some are more complicated. Different cameras take different sizes of film. Yours takes size 110 film.

The camera is a box with a special eye called a "lens," which "sees" only what's in front of it. The camera makes a picture out of whatever it sees.

HANDLE WITH CARE

Cameras are fragile. Be careful not to drop or bang yours. To be safe, always wear the wrist strap and lower the viewfinders when not in use.

Viewfinders

Back door

Film counter window

Shutter button

Wrist strap

Lens

Film advance wheel

The Camera Lens

Beams of light bounce off your "subject" (this is the person or thing you're photographing) and squeeze a picture of it through the lens into the camera. The lens has a cover, called a shutter, that works like an eyelid. It opens and closes in a split second when you press the shutter button (see page 16)—just like the blink of an eye—letting in a tiny bit of light. It's very dark inside the camera—only the light beams carrying your picture can get in. When they do, they put the picture on the film like a movie on a movie screen.

Film

Lens

WHAT A CAMERA SEES

To see the way a camera sees, put your hands on either side of your eyes. A camera sees much less than you do.

If the lens isn't clean, the camera won't be able to see anything. Wipe the lens lightly with a clean cotton swab, but don't touch it with your fingers.

The Film

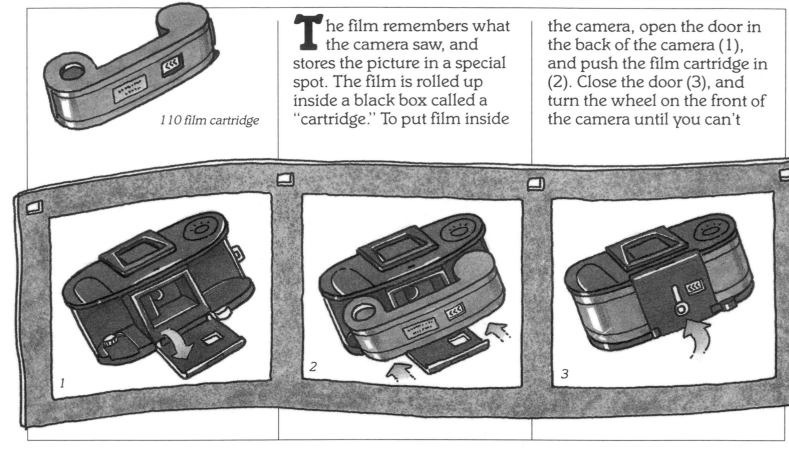

110 film cartridge

The film remembers what the camera saw, and stores the picture in a special spot. The film is rolled up inside a black box called a "cartridge." To put film inside the camera, open the door in the back of the camera (1), and push the film cartridge in (2). Close the door (3), and turn the wheel on the front of the camera until you can't

1

2

3

turn it any more (4). You'll see the number "1" in the window (5), which means you're ready to take your first picture.

Film advance wheel

4

5

Film counter window

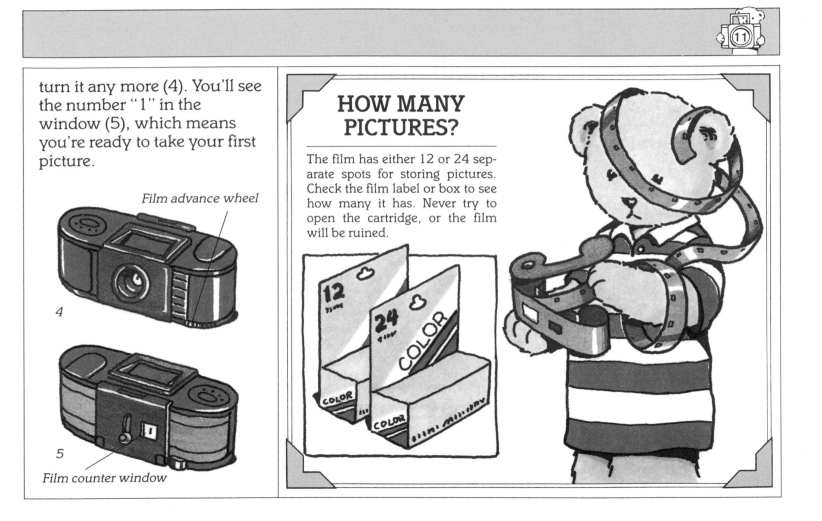

HOW MANY PICTURES?

The film has either 12 or 24 separate spots for storing pictures. Check the film label or box to see how many it has. Never try to open the cartridge, or the film will be ruined.

Holding the Camera

Hold the camera with the lens pointing away from you. This way the lens will see what your eye sees. Hold the camera straight, not tilted forward or sideways. Make sure your finger, hair, or strap doesn't block the lens.

HOLD STILL!

This is the most important rule in photography. Pretend to be a statue if you can.

WHICH BEAR IS HOLDING THE CAMERA CORRECTLY?

Bear #4 is holding the camera correctly.

Viewfinders

Right

Wrong

Lift up the big frame on top of the camera and look through it with one eye. Whatever you see INSIDE this frame (called a "viewfinder") will be in your picture. Don't touch the viewfinder to your eye or the camera will tilt upward. Close your other eye if you can. You can also turn the camera sideways to get a long, tall picture.

When you feel comfortable looking through the big viewfinder frame you may add the small viewfinder frame. Push up on the button in the back door of the camera to raise the small frame. Line up the two frames and look through both of them at the same time. Looking through two frames will help you keep the camera straight, but you only need to use the big frame.

TAKE STEPS

Step forward or back, or move to one side, until you see exactly what you want in your picture.

A button on the back of the camera works the shutter. When you want to take a picture, press the shutter button until you hear a

Shutter button

click, and in a split second the picture will be captured on the film. HOLD STILL while you press the shutter button, and remember to press gently. Don't push so hard that you jiggle the camera or you'll get a blurry picture.

HOLD STILL!

After you've taken your first picture, turn the film advance wheel to wind the film to a new place where no picture has been stored yet.

When you can't turn the wheel any more, the film counter window will read "2." Now you're ready to take your next picture.

OOPS! WHAT WENT WRONG?

When I pressed the shutter button, I jiggled the camera. My subject looks blurry.

When I pressed the shutter button, I pushed the camera so that it pointed in a different direction. My subject is barely there!

The camera needs light in order to see—much more light than you do—so take pictures outside during the day. Try to stand with the sun behind you or to one side of you. Shooting straight into the sun brings too much light into the camera. If you can't see the sun, don't worry, because even a cloudy day can be bright enough for picture taking. Make sure that your subject isn't in shadow. If necessary, move the subject to a brighter spot.

LET THERE BE LIGHT

Which bear is in the best light to be photographed?

Bear #1

Bear #2

Bear #3

Bear #1 is best. Bear #2 is in shadow, and the photographer would have to face into the sun to shoot Bear #3.

Distance

Don't get too close to your subject or your picture will be fuzzy. Take at least two giant steps backward. (Take 10 giant steps back if you're photographing an elephant!) But don't get too far away, either. If it doesn't fill at least half the space in your big viewfinder, the subject will be hard to see in your photograph.

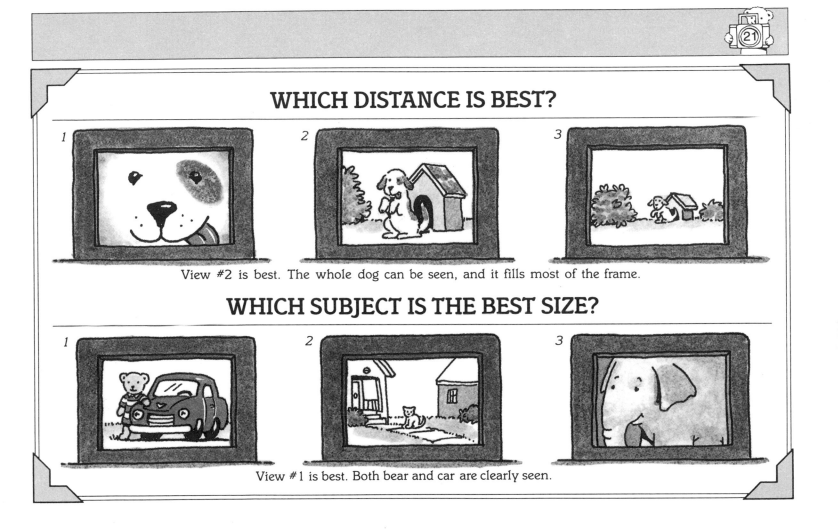

WHICH DISTANCE IS BEST?

View #2 is best. The whole dog can be seen, and it fills most of the frame.

WHICH SUBJECT IS THE BEST SIZE?

View #1 is best. Both bear and car are clearly seen.

Framing and Composition

Look carefully through the viewfinder. Do you see your whole subject? Don't cut off the rabbit's ears or Dad's hat. Don't let a tree grow out

of the top of Mom's head. Put your subject in the middle of the frame. You can shoot a "bird's-eye view" by standing on a step and aiming down at something on the ground. You can shoot a "worm's-eye-view" by lying on the ground and shooting up at something.

WHERE'D SHE GO?

Don't lose your subject by placing her in front of a busy background. A simple background makes your subject easier to see.

Indoor Photography

Although you should take almost all of your snapshots outside with this camera, sometimes you can take a good picture indoors if you follow these rules very carefully: Make sure it's a very bright and sunny day outside; place your subject in a patch of sunlight coming into the room from a window or open door; turn on any lights in the room, but make sure you don't see a lamp or lightbulb in your viewfinder. HOLD STILL—this is even more important than usual. A windowsill with a sleeping cat or pretty flowers is a good subject for indoor photography.

Another way to take pictures indoors is to shoot through a window. This means that your subject is outside, but you are inside. If it's sunny and bright outside, place the camera lens right up against the window glass. Be careful not to jiggle the camera when you press the shutter button. The lens must touch the glass or you might see its reflection along with your subject in the picture.

Processing

When you've turned the film advance wheel as far as it will go and there are no more numbers in the film counter window, you've taken all the pictures the film can hold. Take out the film cartridge, and bring it to the photo shop. Their lab will remove the film from the cartridge and "develop" the pictures on it by dipping the film in chemicals. Then they'll shine light through the film onto special paper. The

pictures stored on the film will appear on the paper. The lab will return your developed film along with the finished photographs. Then you'll be able to see the tiny pictures stored on the strips of film. In order to take more pictures, you'll need a new roll of film.

Making Copies

You can order extra copies of your best pictures to give to friends or to use for projects. You may need an adult's help to find the picture on the film that matches a photograph you want to copy.

The picture on the processed film is called a negative. It will look a little strange because the light and dark parts will be the opposite of those on the photograph. Use the number that appears next to the negative to order copies of the picture you want.

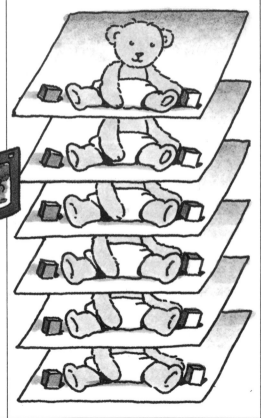

HANDLE WITH CARE

Always pick up film strips by the edges—don't get fingerprints on the film.

If you have a very special picture you want to give as a gift, the photo lab can make an even bigger copy of it for you. Ask an adult to help you choose a picture that's very sharp and clear because the bigger it gets the fuzzier it will look. You won't want to make your copy too big—a little bit bigger will look like a lot. Ask the photo lab what sizes they can make, and remember that enlargements cost more than regular-size pictures.

I Love You Grandpa.

PHOTO ASSIGNMENTS

Professional photographers go out on "photo assignments" to do their work. That means they're going to take a special picture of a person, place, or event. Now that you know how to use your camera, here are some photo assignments for you to try. Always look for these symbols on your assignment pages:

☀	GO OUTSIDE TO A BRIGHT OR SUNNY SPOT
	STAND WITH THE SUN BEHIND OR TO ONE SIDE OF YOU
	TAKE AT LEAST 2 GIANT STEPS BACK FROM YOUR SUBJECT
OOPS	KEEP FINGERS, HAIR, AND CAMERA STRAP FROM BLOCKING THE LENS
HOLD STILL	HOLD STILL WHILE PRESSING THE SHUTTER BUTTON

ASSIGNMENT #1
Portrait

A portrait is a picture of a person. It can show just the head and shoulders, or it can include the whole body. The person can be standing, sitting, or even lying down. Ask your subject to hold or stand next to something important to her or him. Your subject may want to get dressed up in a special outfit for the picture. Ask your subject to HOLD STILL while you press the shutter button.

WHAT'S WRONG WITH THESE PICTURES?

This bear isn't all there!

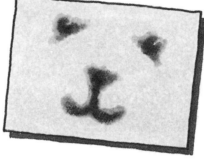

The photographer is too close to the subject.

Is this a portrait? It's hard to tell.

Turn the camera sideways to take a long, tall picture.

When the photographer giggles, the camera jiggles.

This subject is just too far away.

ASSIGNMENT #2
Landscape

A landscape is a picture of the outdoor world. You may find a pretty landscape to shoot while on a trip, or you may want to photograph the street you live on. A picture of big city buildings is called a "cityscape." Look through the viewfinder at the landscape. Is there plenty of light? Can you see some sky at the top of the frame? Are there interesting things to see both far away and closer up? Include part of a fence, tree, or building at the edge of your picture to help make faraway things look VERY far away.

GOOD & BETTER

An empty sky is less interesting than one with clouds, birds, or a rainbow in it.

Adding a person to this picture makes the rocks look even bigger.

Include some interesting objects in the front of your picture.

ASSIGNMENT #3
Still Life

A still life is an arrangement of objects. You've seen lots of still lifes without knowing it. A table set for an outdoor picnic, or the dog's bed, bone, and food bowl—these are still lifes. You can choose objects for a still life because they look nice together and have interesting colors and shapes, or because they have a special meaning for you. Or you can make a "mystery" picture by choosing objects that belong to a special person and have other people guess who that person is. Arrange the objects outside on the ground, a table, step, bench, or chair. Use a scarf or tablecloth for a nice background. Look through the viewfinder—your still life should be in the middle of the frame. Make sure you can see each thing.

Don't use a busy background.

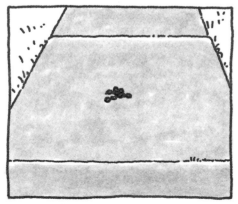

Don't pick tiny things to photograph.

Don't hide important objects.

ASSIGNMENT #4

Group Photo

A group photograph gathers a bunch of people into one picture. You can take a group photograph of your class, your family, or the kids on your block. You can take a group photograph of your pets, too. Look through the viewfinder. Can you see the faces of everyone in the group? Does the group fill up most of the frame? You can arrange your group with some people standing and some sitting or kneeling in front. Try to put the taller people behind and the shorter people in front. Try to get everyone to look at the camera, hold still, and say "cheese" when you press the shutter. (Saying "cheese" makes a person smile.)

DON'T FORGET

OOPS HOLD STILL

TAKING A GROUP PHOTO CAN BE TOUGH!

1. Put smaller subjects in front.
2. Make sure you can see everyone's face.
3. Get the group close together and in the frame.
4. Tell everyone to hold still.
5. Make sure everyone's posed and ready.

ASSIGNMENT #5
Action Photo

In an action photograph, your subject is moving instead of standing still. You can take an action photograph of your father washing the car, your sister throwing a ball, or your dog scratching a flea. If your subject is moving very fast, it will look a little blurry in the picture, but that's okay. You don't have to ask your subject to hold still or smile when you take an action shot—what's important is to capture the action just as you see it.

DON'T FORGET

OOPS

HOLD STILL

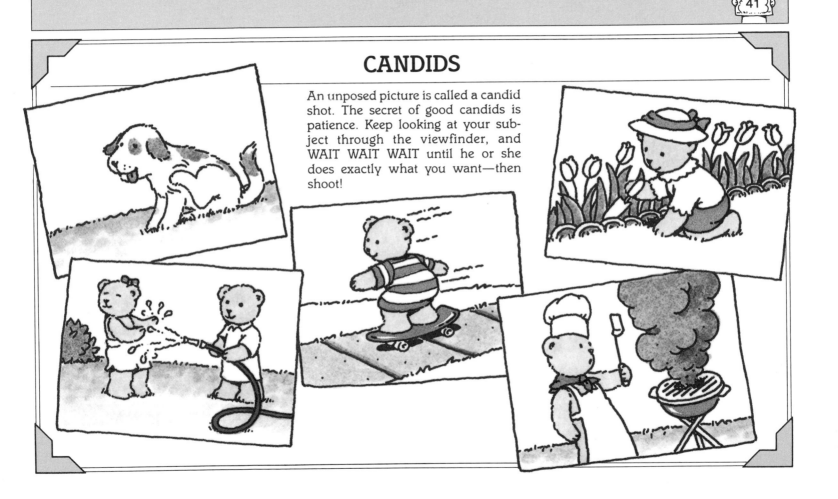

CANDIDS

An unposed picture is called a candid shot. The secret of good candids is patience. Keep looking at your subject through the viewfinder, and WAIT WAIT WAIT until he or she does exactly what you want—then shoot!

ASSIGNMENT #6

Series Photographs

Series photographs are two or more pictures that tell a story. You can make a series of a snowman under construction. You can make a "before-and-after" series of your mother putting on makeup. (Take one picture before she puts on makeup, and one picture after she's all finished.) You can invent a story and shoot a picture to fit each part of your story. You can record your favorite tree as it changes through the seasons. (Take other pictures while you wait.) Plan your series ahead of time so you'll be ready to take the pictures you need. Take lots of pictures, and choose the best ones for the series. Try to make a series that will tell its story without any words.

WHAT STORIES DO THESE SERIES TELL?

DON'T FORGET

OOPS

HOLD STILL

PICTURE PROJECTS

There are wonderful ways to share your photographs with your family and friends. Why not mail a faraway cousin a picture postcard of your dog? Or send him a secret picture puzzle to solve? Or make gifts of framed snapshots that everyone will enjoy? You will need some easy-to-find materials and some help from an adult or older friend to make these projects. Be sure you have lots of pictures to choose from.

Fancy Frames

1 Cut out 3 pieces of cardboard, as shown. Pieces 1 and 2 should be larger than your photo. Make sure the inside hole of the first piece is a little bit smaller than your picture.

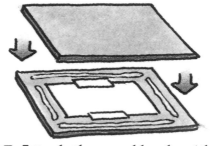

1   2   3

2 Lay the picture, face down, on the first piece, covering the hole. Tape it in place.

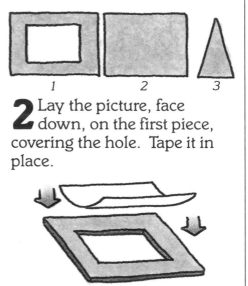

3 Spread paste along each edge of the back of the first piece. Carefully lay the second piece, face up, on top. Clean off any excess paste, and press the frame under a heavy book for 2 hours.

4 Attach the easel back with strips of tape, as shown.

5 Decorate your frame with fancy paper, stickers, glitter, or stamps. Add your initials or a greeting if you like. You can make frames with different-shaped picture openings, or a big frame with openings for several pictures.

Picture Postcards

1 Paste a piece of light-colored construction paper to the back of your picture.

2 Trim off the extra paper with scissors. Press the postcard under a heavy book for 2 hours to keep it flat.

3 Draw a vertical line down the middle of the construction paper. Write your message on the left side, and put the stamp and address on the right side.

Puzzling Pictures

1 Choose a picture with a lot of things in it to make the puzzle more fun. Paste the picture, face up, to a piece of thin cardboard slightly larger than the picture. (Spread lots of paste evenly all over the back of the picture.)

2 Place the picture under a few heavy books for 2 hours so it will dry flat.

3 Trim the cardboard to the picture size.

4 On the cardboard side draw lines, as shown, and carefully cut along these lines to make the puzzle pieces.

5 Shuffle the pieces, and put them in an envelope marked "Solve This!"

Solve This!

Wild Piles

A collage is a picture made of bits and pieces of photos. It's a great way to celebrate a special event, like a birthday—you can use lots of pictures of and about the birthday person.

1 Start with a large piece of plain cardboard and a collection of pictures you might want to use.

2 Cut out the parts of the pictures you like best, such as people, dogs, cars, or trees. Arrange them on the construction paper to make a new picture.

Your collage picture may be funny or silly, or just pretty. Move the pieces around, overlap them a bit, and add a drawn or cut-out background.

3 When you have just what you want, begin pasting down each piece, starting with the pieces underneath and working up to the pieces lying on the top. You can add some drawings in blank spaces, or even words.

MAKING AN ALBUM

A good way to show off your photographs and keep them from getting torn or scratched is to put them in an album. You can use the rest of this book as an album for the best of your pictures. The pages have fun scenes for decoration, and you may find inspiration for new pictures from them: Why not shoot a landscape to paste inside the window frame? Or a beautiful still life to rest on the artist's easel? Don't forget to write down who or what the picture is of, and when you took it. As you grow older, you'll fill many more albums, but you'll still like to look back at your first photographs.

Date:

This is:

Date: This is:

Date: This is:

Date:

This is:

Date: *This is:*

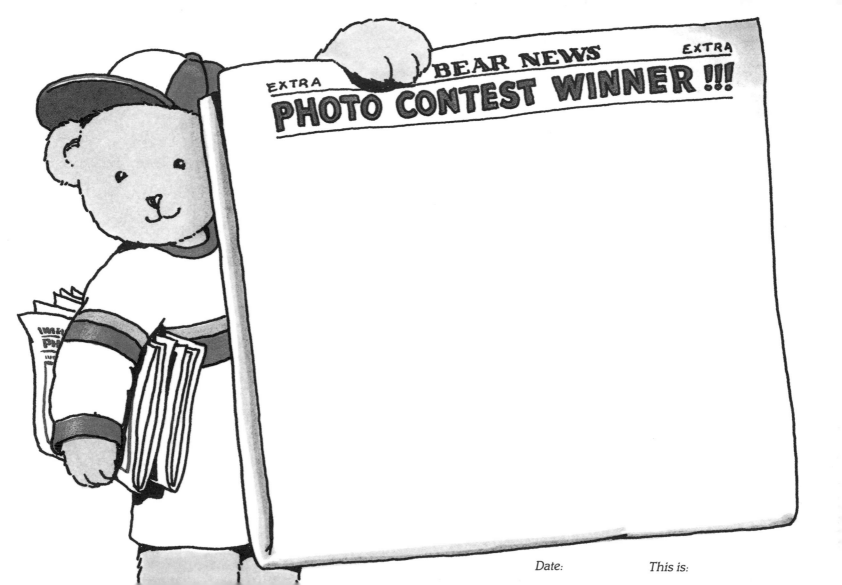

EXTRA · BEAR NEWS · EXTRA

PHOTO CONTEST WINNER !!!

Date: This is:

Date: This is:

Date: This is:

Date:

This is:

Date:

This is:

Date: This is:

Date: This is: